Meet the Mets' Mess

The R-E-G-R-E-T-S of New York Town

Neil Villapiano

Nosebleeds Books

ISBN: 978-0-578-81147-5

Copyright © 2020 Neil Villapiano.
All rights reserved.
No part of this book may be reproduced or transmitted in any form or by any means, electronic or mechanical, including photocopying, recording, or by any information storage and retrieval system, without prior permission in writing from the Author.

Villapiano, Neil
Meet the Mets' Mess/ Neil Villapiano. —1st ed. p. cm.

Printed and Manufactured in the United States of America

Also available as an eBook

Although the 14 chapters of this little tome are reminiscent of that other great 14, Gil Hodges, this book has to be dedicated to the memory of the greatest Met of them all, the man who switched those numbers around, "The Franchise" - the late, great 41, Tom "Terrific" Seaver.

TABLE OF CONTENTS

Introduction: We Gotta Believe? i

Amazin They Still Had a Franchise 2
The Winds of Shea 7
Bumblin' Out of the Gate 11
1969 17
He's Outta Here! 26
Leading Up to the Second "Miracle" 39
1986 45
The Second Miracle 52
Sour Apples 57
A Light - in the "Piazza" 64
2000 70
The Sub (par) Way Series 76
The Decade of Regrets 88
A New Hope...? 96

Epilogue: The R-E-G-R-E-T-S of New York Town 105

Introduction: You Gotta Believe?

It's a cold, clear night at Shea Stadium on October 19th, 2006. 56,357 Mets fans file in to witness Game 7 of the National League Series. The Mets are coming into tonight after a 4-2 victory the night before to force this decisive game. This Mets team dominated the regular season and won the National League East. They breezed through the NLDS and now have home field advantage in the biggest game in franchise history since Game 1 of the 2000 World Series. The whole city of New York is ready for a coronation.

Their opponent on this evening is the St. Louis Cardinals who barely squeaked into the postseason by winning a mere 83 games, a full 14 fewer than the Mets. The Cardinals have Jeff Suppan on the mound who went eight shutout innings in Game 3 in St. Louis to help the Cardinals grab a 2-1 lead in the series. On the bump for the Mets is the young Oliver Perez who they feel will be the key to winning this game. This sure is to be one for the ages. One that Mets fans believe will end, in just a few hours, in the long awaited glory, a World Series berth.

In the bottom of the 1st, after the Cardinals put up zero, Carlos Beltran, who despite having spent so much of his time as an injured Met, had been a nemesis to the Cardinals all series long, gets a 2-out double to give the Mets an opportunity. They pounce on that opportunity 2 batters later when David Wright singles him in to give the Mets an early 1-0 lead. Already Mets can smell it in the air that the night will be theirs - a great night for that coronation in Queens.

Unfortunately, the Cardinals had other plans, in just the very next half inning, in the top of the 2nd, St. Louis gets two singles, putting runners on 1st and 3rd with only 1 out. Second Baseman Ronnie Belliard comes to the plate and lays down a textbook sacrifice bunt to bring in the lead runner and tie the game at 1. This already has the makings of a back and forth duel that may go deep into the October night.

Things actually quiet down for the next several innings until we find ourselves at the top of the 6th inning. At this point, any play, any at-bat, any pitch, could be the decisive factor in the outcome. After Jim Edmonds works a one out walk, up steps Scott Rolen, who has struggled at the plate in this playoff year. However on the first pitch he sees, he rips one deep to left field. Mets fans hold their breath. NO! NOT NOW! The ball is going, going, and it is...CAUGHT!

WHAT!?!?

Endy Chavez, the Mets left fielder had leapt over the wall and robbed a home run! He throws the ball back into the infield and the Mets get a double play out of the deal because Jim Edmonds was halfway to third thinking that ball was on its way out. Mets fans go insane! They can't believe the play that Chavez just made, saving two runs and possibly the entire game, to say nothing of the season. In a split second, the Mets had all the momentum they needed in the game and were poised to take that momentum into the bottom half of the inning.

In that frame, the Mets load the bases after 2 walks and an error. Stepping up to the plate is Jose Valentin with only one out. This is the moment that Mets fans had been waiting for: The chance to firmly grab the lead and bury any hope the Cardinals may have left in this contest. Valentin, working on a 5 pitch at-bat however, strikes out swinging on an off-speed pitch inside.

Next up - the man of the hour, Endy Chavez, who just saved those two crucial runs in the top of the frame can now give the Mets the lead in the bottom, and be the hero once more!

The first pitch is right down the freaking middle. OH! It's perfect! Chavez, with all his might swings at it, hits in the air...right to Jim Edmonds in medium center field to end the inning. A little demoralizing for the Mets and their fans. However, the home team still had the momentum and the home crowd behind them. Plus, still two innings to go – and the all-important last ups. Everything will work out in the end , right? This is still their time, right?

Both teams settle down again and it seems like we might be heading for extra innings to decide this one. Then, we go to the top of the 9th. With both starters already done for the game, it's up to the bullpens to finish this one out. Jim Edmonds leads off the inning striking out and then Scott Rolen gets a one out single to left. This brings up St. Louis' young phenom catcher, Yadier Molina. Mets pitcher Aaron Heilman nods to catcher Paul Lo Duca and delivers the pitch. BOP! A drive to deep left field. NO! NOT NOW! Wait it's Chavez again, he'll catch another one and save the day again! The ball is going, going, and it is...GONE! What?

WHAT!?!?

Cardinals 3 Mets 1 going to the bottom of the 9th...

The Mets however, don't go quietly into the New York night. Jose Valentin and Endy Chavez lead off the inning with back-to-back singles. Then, after two quick outs, Paul Lo Duca works a walk. That brings up the very dangerous...Carlos Beltran. Isn't this perfect Mets fans? The most clutch hitter on the Mets, and maybe in the entire game of baseball, is up with the bases loaded and a chance not only to tie the game, but with an extra base hit, send the Mets to the Fall Classic.

Cardinals rookie closer Adam Wainwright knows that this will be a daunting task ahead of him. The first pitch is a changeup down the middle. Beltran lets it go. Strike one. Pitch two is a curveball in the dirt, Beltran swings and misses. Strike two. Mets fans holding their collective breath - they still have hope, this will all work out, the Mets will win! Wainwright comes to set, he's ready, Beltran is ready. The wind up and the 0-2 pitch…

"Oh, somewhere in this favored land the sun is shining bright;
The band is playing somewhere, and somewhere hearts are light,
And somewhere men are laughing, and somewhere children shout; But there is no joy in Flushing…"

That one at-bat crystallizes what is has been like to be a fan of the Mets for years – with few exceptions, since their inception. They become very good, they bring joy and hopefulness. They make you believe that this will be the year. That all will be forgiven and the Mets will become champions once again. They get oh so close…then it all falls apart. This makes every year more and more agonizing. When will it end? Why does it happen to us? What did we do – or not do – to deserve this?

1
Amazin' They Still Had a Franchise

Once upon a time there were three professional baseball that thrived in New York City and it seemed like they would stay that way forever. Unfortunately in 1957, New York baseball took a major hit. Both of the city's National League teams - the Brooklyn Dodgers and New York Giants - left the city for the sunnier climes of California. Now, only one team, the Yankees, was left. This was a massive shock to the city - not every New Yorker was a Yankee fan; in fact, the fans of the city's former National League teams could be counted among the "haters". For so many of those fans, it felt like their very heart had been ripped out. For New York City

Mayor Robert F. Wagner, this problem needed urgent fixing. Later that year, Wagner appointed a 4-man commission to try to get National League baseball back in The Big Apple. One of the men appointed for this was Mr. William "Bill" Shea.

On July 27th 1959, Shea announced the formation of... The Continental Baseball League! It would be a new league with five teams starting play in 1961. One of the teams of the proposed brave new league would be placed in New York City. However, this proposal – the team AND the league - didn't last long. On August 2nd of 1960 the CL disbanded. All was not lost, however. In its stead, Major League Baseball announced that four new franchises, originally proposed as CL teams, would be created as expansion franchises in the existing Major Leagues: two in the "junior circuit", the American League; and two in the National League. One of those NL teams would be slated for New York, to make up for the two teams the City had lost, the now Los Angeles Dodgers and San Francisco Giants. A few months later, on October 17th 1960, the New York Metropolitans were officially added to the National League.

Joan Payson, the team's original owner, decided upon the name of the franchise, perhaps inspired by a similarly named team of the 19th Century. On May 8th of that year, New York's National League club was introduced as the "New York Metropolitan Baseball Club, Inc", with the more fan friendly nickname, the "Mets".

Thus were The New York Mets born, an exciting time for the city of New York and the fans! All of a sudden, there was new life and excitement around having National League baseball back in the Big Apple! Yankee great, Casey Stengel was brought in to be the first manager of the ball club. For many fans at the time, this was an auspicious sign of things to come! Unfortunately, aside from the celebration over the novelty of the return of National League baseball to the city, there wasn't much else to celebrate. From 1962 through 1968, the Mets delivered to their fans 5 seasons of one hundred losses or more while also setting a new standard for ineptitude. With a record like that, it truly was "amazin'" they still had a franchise…

Such a new team would of course need a new stadium – but while it would be under construction, the Mets agreed to play their first two years at the drafty old Polo Grounds in far northern Manhattan, the site which had just been abandoned by the fleeing Giants, and right across the East River from the House that Ruth Built, home of the more established Yankees. When the Mets took over the Polo Ground, they decided to make some changes. The biggest was to redefine the dimensions of the park itself. Other changes were downright "spooky." The Mets wanted to get away from the Ghosts of the NL franchises that had abandoned the city just a few years before. Some great memories like Pafko at the wall, Willie Mays' miraculous catch and others were to be officially wiped away. Even with doing those things, the team was still reminded of the past all the time. They needed their own place, a place where they could call home to create their own identity…

2

The Winds of Shea

Ground was broken for a new stadium in late October of 1961, even as the Mets were making new (if regrettable) memories in the Polo Grounds, their temporary home while they waited. It would be named Shea Stadium, after William Shea, the man that, after all, had brought National League baseball back to New York City. Setting the example of so many particularly (but not exclusively) National League parks to come in the 60s and 70s (think of Veterans Stadium in Philadelphia and Three Rivers, in Pittsburgh), Shea Stadium would be a round stadium. Such a design, though derided by some as "cookie cutter", reflected the bold spirit of the other big development in New York of the time, The World's Fair. Everything seemed possible - the world was entering a new era of futuristic technological advances. The Mets, trying to catch this forward-looking wave, adopted the Fair's color scheme, just as the city had done. But more importantly, the Mets colors gave homage to the previous NL teams in New York, which had so recently abandoned the city and their local fans: The blue was a tribute to the Brooklyn Dodgers and the orange was a nod to the New York Giants.

With such bright changes, the Mets hoped to show that there would be a new age dawning in New York City. Not just for baseball, but for the city itself. The beginning of what everyone hoped would be something special. One could feel the winds of change sweeping across the land…

It's fair to say that the winds of Shea Stadium have not always been kind to the home team. In fact, they seem to be more favorable to everyone else BUT them. When Shea was built in 1964, Mayor Wagner called it "one of the most modern and beautiful sports facilities in the world." But the allure of the place seemed to fade by just its third year. Many criticized the stadium itself as nothing more than soullessly symmetrical. The seats in the stadium, which reflected the teams new color scheme, sported colors that literally were "not found in nature." (Years later, when I went to Citi Field for the first time, the person I was with - who had been to Shea many times - upon entering the new stadium, looked around in amazement and said, "wow…the seats are a normal color!") Being right near Flushing Bay, it had one thing in common with the now San Francisco Giants' new but similarly soulless, symmetrical and ill-positioned Candlestick Park.

And then, of course, were the neighbors…roaring LaGuardia Airport was bad enough, but there also were many automobile junkyards and "chop shops" just beyond the parking lot. Shea became noisy and dingy very quickly - symbolizing what it would be like to be a fan of this team for many swirling, dirty, cacaphonous years to come.

The wind. It was fierce and unpredictable in April, making it extremely difficult to play in, to say the least. There is the famous shot of the end zone flags from an NFL playoff game in December 1968 (involving Shea co-tenants, the NY Jets) where the winds of Shea made them be stiffly pointing at each other, rather than both reflecting a common wind patter in one direction or the other, where both flags pointed to the right or to the left. That indicated the problem of the swirling winds. It was also really bad in October…although the Mets didn't play much October baseball those days. The reason for not playing any October baseball is much more painful than anyone might had thought at first…

3

Bumblin' Out of the Gate (Hell Gate)

On a good day, from the upper decks of Shea, you could see a bridge that many have come to know as the Hell Gate Bridge. The Hell Gate Bridge, originally the New York Connecting Railroad Bridge or the East River Arch Bridge, is a 1,017-foot (310 m) steel through arch railroad bridge in New York City. It got its name from being placed above the Hell Gate Strait. Just like the bridge's towers, the Mets in The Polo Grounds, where you could also see Hell Gate, served very little to no purpose in the first few years of the franchise's existence.

And speaking of gates (and "hell" gate at that), the team hired Yankee great Casey Stengel to be the first manager in team history and hoped he would get the team off on the right foot, right out of the gate. However, "The Old Perfessor" wasn't the only one who was old. The Mets teams from 1962-1965 had 16 players that were 30 years or older. Frank Thomas (33), Richie Ashburn (35), Brooklyn Dodger great Gil Hodges (38) and Giants great Roger Craig (32) were some of the older players on those clubs. The team hoped those big (if faded) names would garner some new fans to the games as the fledgling team garnered some wins in the standings.

The Mets needed to bring in a star to help and thought they had done just that in their inaugural season. On May 9th, 1962, the team acquired Marv Throneberry from the Orioles, a man who had flourished in the mid-to-late Fifties. He had led the American Association (the original Minor League) in home runs and RBI's for three straight seasons ('55-'57). His performance got him a chance to rejoin the Yankees, the team that originally drafted him, in 1958. By the time he arrived in the Blue and Orange (the Mets' team colors, derived from the Giants orange and the Dodgers blue), however, Throneberry was struggling to find his game and was a bit older, (to say the least!). The Mets and their fans were expecting big things from "Marvelous Marv"! What they got instead was anything but.

It's probably safe to say that from the perspective of Mets fans, this trade was the WORST move in franchise history, to that point, anyway. Throneberry had never been considered a great fielder, but he had made up for that deficiency with left-handed power - when he was with the Yanks. When he got to Shea, however, everything imploded. He made some of the most stupefying mistakes (the most errors in one season by any player) and whatever those mistakes might have lacked in differentiation, he made up for with quantity. Throneberry started 89 games at first base, totaling up 779 1/3 innings…WITH 17 ERRORS ALL BY HIMSELF.

But perhaps no play best describes the poor play of Throneberry than the events of June 17th, 1962. The Mets were playing at the Polo Grounds in a double-header vs. the Chicago Cubs. The Mets were down 4-1 in the bottom of the first inning when Throneberry hit a ball into the right-center field gap, a triple that drove in 2 runs to cut the deficit to just one run. However, he was called out because he had somehow missed touching first base. HOW THE HECK DOES THAT HAPPEN!?!? When manager Casey Stengel came out to argue, he was stopped by first-base coach (and former Dodger) Cookie Lavagetto, who was quoted as saying, "Don't bother, Case, he didn't touch second either."

Unreal. Stengel, as well as, Mets fans really began to wonder, "Can anybody here play this game"?

Throneberry would later become a spokesperson for Miller Lite, noting, "If I do for Lite what I did for baseball, I'm afraid their sales would go down".

Whatever the case was for Miller, it certainly was the case for the Mets while he was there. He dropped pop ups, misplayed easy grounders and his throwing was, for the most part, just awful. Of course, the Throneberry acquisition would prove to be just the first in a long list of questionable moves this franchise would make.

Speaking of pop_ups, there is one play that many of the older Mets fans will remember, or better yet, would like to forget. During the inaugural 1962 season, Richie Ashburn and shortstop Elio Chacón continuously collided with each other in the outfield. The problem was that Ashburn would yell, "I got it! I got it!" only to run into Chacón, who spoke only Spanish. Ashburn learned to yell, "¡Yo la tengo! ¡Yo la tengo!" instead. This worked well for a while. But in another game later that season, while Chacón backed off as he yelled "¡Yo la tengo!", Ashburn easily positioned himself to catch the ball, a pop up to shallow left. But although their new found multilingual communication averted a collision with Chacón, Ashburn was instead run over by left fielder Frank Thomas, who understood no Spanish! Apparently Thomas had missed the team meeting about using the Spanish phrase to avoid outfield collisions. After the two had gotten up, Thomas asked Ashburn in no uncertain terms, "What the heck is a Yellow Tango"?

That same miscommunication would become emblematic of many Mets moves yet to come. Moves that would leave Mets fans screaming "NO la tengo!". Stengel didn't stick around; he was so tired of the losing - and the team was so tired of him – that they mutually agreed that he should retire after the '65 season. Understandable, given those 5 first seasons of 100+ losses. They looked like they were never going to win…

But then…A MIRACLE OCCURRED. ..

4

1969

At the start of the '68 season, the Mets really needed to find SOME way to gain respectability around baseball - to say nothing of the city of New York, for that matter. Through all the seasons of their brief existence, the Mets had failed to have even one winning season - and were dubbed by the New York press "Lovable Losers". "Lovable" might have been acceptable; "Losers" definitely was not! President John F. Kennedy had said in September of 1962 - the Mets inaugural year - that we as a country were going to put a man on the moon. Some people thought he was crazy to say that. If he had instead proclaimed that the Mets would win a World Series, the whole country would have thought he had really lost it. While NASA was approaching the feat they had set out to achieve, the Mets still needed to figure out the ground work for their own launch.

By '67, the Mets had been able to acquire some really good talent that could take them to places beyond in the baseball universe, particularly three dominant arms in the pitching staff. There was Jerry Koosman, a talented southpaw who would become a great complement to the strong right handers they were also acquiring. One of those right handers was a fellow who would prove to be one of the greatest pitchers in baseball history, someone named Nolan Ryan from Texas that no one seemed to be able to get a hit off of.

And then of course, there was a recent USC grad, a kid by the name of Tom Seaver, who had become available after an early agreement he had made with the Atlanta Braves was voided by MLB.

The Mets organization, also needing a new manager, knew they had to bring in a younger voice who understood what it took to win. They did just that in 1968 by trading $100,000 and pitcher Bill Denehy to the Washington Senators for Brooklyn Dodger great (and former Met), Gil Hodges. (Yes, despite how young the franchise was, there was such a thing as a "former Met"...) With Hodges at the helm, the team improved significantly that season, going 73-89. They finished 9th in the National League, only a slight improvement but even still their best season to date. His style of "tough, but fair" was going to be especially vital going into '69.

The Mets were projected to finish in dead last in the new NL East Division that year, even behind the first year Montreal Expos. The projections seemed accurate at first, when the Mets dropped their opening game 11-10 to those aforementioned Expos and by the time June rolled around, the Mets were still poking around at just under .500. But when they rolled off 11 consecutive wins, people took notice. All they needed to do now was overtake the talented Chicago Cubs (skippered by NY City legend Leo Durocher) for the division lead…

It would all come to a head in a handful of matchups between the two teams throughout the summer, with the Mets for the most part, winning those games. Unfortunately, the Cubs still had an almost 10 game lead on the Mets in mid-August. Many believed that the Mets would flounder down the stretch - "Lovable Losers", right? - the same team that couldn't get out of last place in any way up until that point. Then…things began to change!

The Mets dominated the rest of that regular season winning 38 of the final 49 games with two big wins vs. the Cubs in early September. That started a 10-game winning streak pushing the Mets into first place. They clinched the NL East in their final home game - luckily, and to the great satisfaction of their fans, just before a week-long, season-ending road trip.

1969

They had done it! The Mets were winners for the first time ever! And not just winners, but DIVISION WINNERS! You could even say that it was "Amazin", as the NY media market abandoning the moniker "Lovable Losers", began calling them - the Amazins! They finished the year 100-62 and were off to the postseason. The Mets faced the Atlanta Braves in the NLCS and behind timely hitting, prevailed. All of a sudden the Mets were in the World Series!

It truly WAS "Amazin"!

Their opponent in the Fall Classic was an intimidating juggernaut of a team - The Baltimore Orioles - that seemed unbeatable. Led by the great manager Earl Weaver, the O's had become a dominant force in the American League. They had won 109 games that season, their first under his tutelage, and were primed for a championship. The team was a hitting machine with Boog Powell and the Robinson "brothers", Frank and

Brooks, leading the way. Their pitching staff was also incredible, with Dave McNally and Jim Palmer. The Orioles dominated the ALCS, sweeping the Minnesota Twins aside in three straight. Clearly the Mets were considered the underdogs going into this Series, if not sacrificial lambs.

It definitely looked that way after the O's beat Tom Seaver 4-1 in Game 1. However, these Mets would not give up so easily. Jerry Koosman was brilliant in the bounce-back Game 2, getting the first 18 batters out to secure a hard won 2-1 victory. The Mets had won the first World Series game in their history! The next three games were to be played in New York. The momentum was shifting in the Mets favor. In Game 3, Gary Gentry and Nolan Ryan were great on the mound. The biggest story of the game however was Tommie Agee, who single-handedly robbed several runs from the Orioles with great catches in the outfield. The Mets earned a 5-0 victory, taking a 2-1 lead in the Series.

In Game 4, Tom Seaver was back to his brilliant self as he went the distance in another close 2-1 victory. All of a sudden, the Mets were just one win away from winning the World Series! ONE! With a chance to win it at Shea! The Orioles started off with a 3-0 lead in Game 5, looking to send the series back to Baltimore. Then everything changed, when the Orioles' Frank Robinson appeared to be hit by a Koosman pitch—only to have it ruled a foul ball off his bat by home plate umpire Lou DiMuro. Robinson finished the at-bat by striking out. In the Mets' half of the sixth, a pitch to Cleon Jones seemed to elude him. However, DiMuro actually decided, in that instance, that Jones WAS hit and gave him the base. Donn Clendenon then clubbed a 2-run homer to cut the deficit to one. Just like that, the tide had changed. The Mets went on to score three more runs in the late innings to take a 5-3 lead going into the 9th.

Meet the Mets' Mess

The last Baltimore out was made by none other than Davey Johnson (who seventeen years later would lead the Mets to their next World Series victory) and the "Miracle Mets" were World Series Champions! Nobody could believe that this had actually happened! It truly was a miracle! "Lovable Losers" no more! All those early years of 100 losses now seemed as far away as the moon!

This team must have gotten some magic from "Broadway Joe" Namath after their stadium-mates, the New York Jets, won Super Bowl III in January '69 (subsequently, the Mets, would pass it on to the Knicks who went on to win the NBA championship in 69-70)! After honoring the Apollo 11 astronauts and the Jets winning the Super Bowl, New York City, for the third time in 8 months, had a ticker-tape parade. - This time it was for their other-worldly team - THE AMAZIN' MIRACLE METS OF 1969!

The bells rang out loud and clear after that miracle

1969

season!

Unfortunately, they were not wedding bells…

5

"He's Outta Here!"

You would've thought that after '69 the Mets would have begun a long run of dominance, not just in the National League, but in the entirety of Major League Baseball, for years to come. What Mets fans got instead was a long run of the talent that they put together - slowly but surely - being kicked to the curb. By the end of the 1971 season the "Miracle" had gone away. The team had back-to-back 83-79 records, not even sniffing the World Series. Mets general manager Bob Scheffing felt that it was time to start making changes. So, on December 10, 1971...The Mets traded away Nolan Ryan.

Let that sink in. Nolan Ryan. The great Hall of Famer to be. Nolan Ryan. The man who would go on to throw seven no hitters (not one for the Mets).

"He's Outta Here!"

Nolan. Ryan…

Unfortunately for Mets fans, who were having great trouble letting it sink in, the Mets front office felt that they had given the young 24 year old every chance to take the next step. But by that point, although Ryan had shown flashes of brilliance, he never showed it consistently. So Scheffing gave up and dealt Ryan, as well as three prospects to the California Angels (who later became the Los Angeles Angels) for 6-time American League All Star Jim Fregosi. Even though the Mets had given up a lot, most people felt that this deal would be more of an advantage to the Mets than the Angels. Many felt that Fregosi would be a Met for a long time…Oh how wrong they were!

Fregosi suited up for the Blue and Orange for only the 1972 and '73 seasons - a season he did not complete with the Mets. He finished with just 150 hits and batted about .230 before being traded midway through the '73 season to the Texas Rangers.

And what happened to Nolan Ryan? Well, he blossomed almost immediately after the trade, becoming a 19-game winner with 329 strikeouts and a remarkable 2.28 ERA in 1972 and throwing 4 no hitters for the Angels alone. He would go on to pitch 3 more no hitters before finally hanging up the spikes in 1993, becoming one of the greatest pitchers of all time with a lifetime record of 324–292 (. 526). He was an eight-time MLB All-Star. His 5,714 career strikeouts is an MLB record by a significant margin. Oh, and did I forget to mention, he also made it to the Baseball Hall of Fame?

To show you how much the Mets goofed on the right hander, here is a quote from Mets GM Bob Scheffing on why he made the deal, "We've had him three full years and although [he was] a hell of a prospect, he hasn't done if for us,'' he told the New York Times after the deal. "How long can you wait? I don't rate him in the same category with Tom Seaver, Jerry Koosman or Gary Gentry."

Yeah, it's safe to say that the Mets clearly didn't see what they had in Ryan and it has haunted them to this day. But the haunting didn't stop there!

For then there was Jerry Koosman, who would pitch a handful more years in the Big Apple. He continued to pitch well, helping the Mets get back to the World Series in 1973 (with Willie Mays in center as well, even though he was long past his prime by then). However, after a 3–15 season in 1978 Koosman, seeing no improvement by the team any time soon, was traded to the Minnesota Twins at his request. You have to understand, the Mets had done so little to make the team better that Koosman basically gave up and wanted out. This was much like a lot of Mets fans at that time, even though when Koosman finally retired, he would still have the third most wins in Mets history (140).

Meet the Mets' Mess

But in the middle of those two haunting disasters, the Mets made the worst trade in their history BY FAR. It would be a move that Mets fans still try to forget, but can't. It continues to torment them to this very day.

By 1976, Tom Seaver was no doubt, the best pitcher in all of baseball. He had just earned his third Cy Young award the previous year, which was his second in three years. He went 22-9 with an impressive 2.38 ERA. Seaver had taken a pay cut in '75 by his own request, because he wanted to prove he deserved more money. And boy he did just that!

Unfortunately, for Mets fans, ownership did not feel the same way. There was a contract dispute between the two sides and for the first of many times, the Mets did not want to spend top dollar on a player. What a shocker. Instead, the Mets decided to make the move that would later mar their franchise for years to come.

It looked like Seaver was going to go to the Dodgers.

Then a report from the Newark Star Ledger came out that he was being traded to LA for another Hall of Famer in Don Sutton. However, the rule back then was, because Sutton had one more year of service than Tom Seaver, he had made it to the ten-year threshold and had the right to refuse any trade. To few people's surprise, Sutton didn't want to be a Met. (Wags said, "Who would want to??"). The deal fell through and the Mets kept Seaver in '76. He had a decent year, but not at the level he was accustomed to having. So, a year and a half later, the Mets finally did trade Seaver in the now infamous "Midnight Massacre" to the Cincinnati Reds in exchange for Pat Zachry, Doug Flynn, Steve Henderson and Dan Norman. Truly, a dark day in Mets history.

Seaver would go on to become the highest paid pitcher in history, at the time. He would also become one of the greatest pitchers ever. Seaver DID however come back to the Mets in 1983, but by that time his best days were far behind him. He had a 9–14 record that season. The Mets exercised an option on Seaver's contract worth $750,000 for the 1984 season. During a 20-year MLB career, he compiled 311 wins, 3,640 strikeouts, 61 shutouts, and a 2.86 earned run average. He would go on to be inducted into the baseball Hall of Fame just like his teammate Nolan Ryan.

...

A special word about Seaver...

Tom "Terrific" Seaver WAS "The Franchise." Thus no one in their wildest dreams could ever imagine that Seaver of all people would be cast away by the Mets - He WAS the Mets, the Hero of the Miracle Year, 1969. Trading him would not only mean losing arguably the greatest pitcher of his generation (and certainly the most clutch), but losing the heart and soul of the franchise - and of the fanbase. Many Mets fans, including ESPN Radio's Don LaGreca, will tell you that trading Tom Seaver away was the biggest, most gut-wrenching regret that fans of the team ever experienced. It is pain that will not forget, that falls drop by drop upon the Mets' fan's heart, as Aeschylus would have put it. It was that big of a deal. He was everything to the Mets fans.

When Citi Field opened, there was a lot of hue and cry over the fact that the lobby of the entrance was dedicated to Jackie Robinson, a Brooklyn Dodger. Many Mets fans and alums alike wanted the team to honor Seaver instead. Finally (some would say grudgingly), in late June of 2019, the Mets finally did "Tom Terrific" right by naming the street outside the stadium Seaver Way. Even doing that could not make the fans forget what the team had done to its favorite son.

What made the deal even worse was what happened after Seaver accomplished major milestones. First, he reached 300 career wins…in another uniform! Then, he threw a no-hitter in Yankee Stadium (yay)…in another uniform (boo)! The last one hurt the most for not just for Mets fans, but Seaver himself. He finally made it back to the Big Dance in 1986...But (you guessed it) in another uniform and had to watch his former team celebrate its first championship since when Seaver brought the City its first since the miracle of 17 years earlier. He should've been a Met still, but instead he was on the other side, in agony.

What made that move particularly galling was that Seaver was in his prime. He was the best pitcher in the game and well on his way to a Hall of Fame career. The Mets took a long time to recover from that move. It was the Great Sin, not forgotten by any Mets fan. One diehard I know even gave up being a Mets fan and became, of all things, a Yankees fan! Mets fans not even born at the time of the trade carry the hurt. It will never go away. The R-E-G-R-E-T will never die.

...

"He's Outta Here!"

The Seaver move put the Mets back for at least a decade before they could recover. Now, of all the players from that magical run of 1969 were gone. All except one. I don't think anyone would guess who would be the only player to remain on the team for his entire career. That man is non-other than Ed, "Freaking" Kranepool. Kranepool had come to the Mets in 1962 and played his entire career up until 1979 with the Blue and Orange. He finished with a .261 Batting Average, 118 Home Runs, and 614 RBI's. The man was never moved or even considered to be moved at any point in his career. Think about that! This team had arguably two of the greatest pitchers of all time on the same team, traded them both away for basically nothing, but never got an offer or wanted an offer for ED KRANEPOOL!?!?

You can't make this stuff up!

Ed actually became the most forever guy in Mets history. Of all the great players the Mets have had on

Meet the Mets' Mess

their team, it's Ed Kranepool who lasted the longest. It became so unbelievable, that ESPN 98.7's Don LaGreca went on a several minute rant on The Michael Kay Show about how the Mets have only one forever guy:

"Who's the forever guy? Ed Kranepool? And they treated him badly, too." "When David Wright was breaking every offensive record, he was breaking Ed Kranepool's records, Michael, - ED KRANEPOOL!" "Not Ruth, not Gehrig, not Mantle, not Dimaggio, not Berra, not Jeter, not Pettite, not Andujar, not Torres, not Judge, not Bird...ED KRANEPOOL! ED KRANEPOOL!" "There's ninety percent of this audience right now that couldn't pick Ed Kranepool out of a lineup. If Ed Kranepool picked them up at the airport, they would say," "hey dude what's your name? Can you take me to midtown? You played for the Mets? That's cool man! When did play for the Mets? That's awesome dude!" "THAT'S YOUR FOREVER GUY! ED...BLEEPIN'

KRANEPOOL!" "THAT'S IT! THERE'S NOT ONE OTHER ONE! NOT ONE!"

It's safe to say Ed Kranepool was not the player that Mets fans had hoped would be their "Forever" guy.

It looked like the Mets would never be able to bring back any sort of the hope or belief that made them "gotta believe" - that they could one day be champions again…

Meet the Mets' Mess

6
Leading Up to the Second "Miracle"

By 1983, the Mets "miracle magic" had been long gone. Oh, sure, the team had gotten back to the World Series in 1973, but they lost in heartbreaking fashion in seven games to the Oakland Athletics of early 70s dynasty fame. Many fans believed that this would be the beginning of a resurgence of the franchise. However, once the main core of the club had left (Tom Seaver, Jerry Koosman, Nolan Ryan and others) they entered into a very dark period of their history. One, they feared, that might even be worse than before '69.

From 1974 to 1983, the Mets would have 8 losing seasons, including only 41 wins in the strike-shortened season of 1981. They tried to bring some of that "magic" back when new ownership reacquired Tom Seaver from the Reds before the start of the '83' season. But they left him unprotected in the expansion draft of 1984, as part of the Player Compensation Pool. Seaver would go on to win his 300th game in New York...it just wasn't with the Mets, it was the White Sox, and it wasn't at Shea Stadium, but at YANKEE STADIUM!

That was the low point for Mets fandom. Fans wondered if the team would truly ever get back to any sort of relevance...Then, as if it was 1968 again, things began to take a turn for the better!

By the start of the 1983 season, the Mets clearly did not have the talent at the big league club to be competitive at all. However, down on the farm in the minor leagues the team organization was building a very special group of players.

The first was a pitcher from Hawaii who had starred at Yale University. His name was Ron Darling, originally drafted by the Texas Rangers in '81, but then traded the following year to the Mets for Lee Mazzilli. Despite the fact that Darling had control problems with his pitches, he was called up in 1983 and became a very reliable starter for a struggling Mets team at the time.

The other was a phenomenal hitter whose swing was as sweet as his last name - Darryl Strawberry. Strawberry was born in Los Angeles, California and it was immediately clear that he was a superstar in the making. Chosen first overall in the 1980 Major League Baseball draft by the New York Mets, Strawberry rose rapidly through the Mets system. He employed a distinctive batting stance with a high leg kick, reached the major league level in 1983, posting 26 home runs, 7 triples, and 74 runs batted in, while hitting for a .257 average. He was named the National League's Rookie of The Year in 1983 and the following year, he once again hit 26 home runs, this time driving in 97 runs, good enough to make the first of 8 consecutive appearances in the All-Star game.

Clearly, the Mets had found some gems. But even still, the best was yet to come.

The team knew they needed an ace of the pitching rotation - someone who could carry the load and perform on the biggest stage in all of sports - New York City. They would find just that someone in a kid from Tampa, Florida with the stuff of which legends are made. Of course, that would be the one, the only, Dwight Gooden, a phenom pitcher who was drafted in the first round in 1982. He spent one season in the minors, in which he led the Class-A Carolina League in wins, strikeouts and ERA while playing for the Lynchburg Mets. He was so good in fact, that he was called up to play for the Mets' AAA team, the Tidewater Tides, during their postseason. By 1984, he had made the major league starting rotation and "Dr. K" showed the world what he could do.

Gooden would go an amazing 17-9 record in his rookie

year, make the All Star team and receive Rookie of The Year honors - the second Met in as many years. In '85, he would become even more unreal as he went 24-4 with a 1.53 ERA en route to winning his first National League Cy Young Award. The Mets had found their ace!

To this tremendous core, the Mets would add from their farm system other guys to the fold such as Lenny Dykstra, Roger McDowell and Sid Fernandez. They would also acquire both Keith Hernandez and Gary Carter via trades. They finally had the pieces in place, they just needed the right man at the helm to right the ship. Like with Gil Hodges, the Mets found their man in Davey Johnson (remember '69!?) who had gone from player to manager in the Mets farm system before being hired by the big league club in 1984.

The team would have a solid season in 1984 with 90 wins as well as a second-place finish. The rise continued in 1985, as they got 98 wins and finished the season only

3 games behind the St. Louis Cardinals. Before the start of the 1985–86 season, general manager Frank Cashen knew the team needed a few more pieces. So, he went out and got Tim Teufel, a right-handed hitting infielder from the Minnesota Twins, and Bob Ojeda, a left-handed pitcher from the Boston Red Sox. The Mets added them along with former MVP outfielder George Foster and speedsters Wally Backman and Mookie Wilson.

The team was now primed for a championship run. So much so that Davey Johnson said to his players that they were not only going to win, but that they would dominate.

7

1986

They would do just that in 1986, winning 108 games, a club record that stands to this day - for a win ratio of two out of every three. They finished the year 21 1/2 games in front of the second place Philadelphia Phillies. It was truly "amazin'"!

They would match up with the Houston Astros in the NLCS against a familiar face - former-Met Nolan Ryan, who by that point had become one of the best pitchers in the game - to say nothing of the great Mike Scott. The Mets knew they would have their hands full. Not surprisingly, they were named the clear underdogs in the series. The teams had traded wins going into Game 6. The Mets were up, 3 games to 2, having won every game in which Mike Scott did not pitch, with the series going

Meet the Mets' Mess

back to Houston. What followed would be a 16-inning thriller that saw the Mets score 3 runs in the top of the 16th to take a 7-4 lead. However, in the bottom half of the frame, the Astros scored 2 runs in the humid Texas night to pull within 1. But pitcher Jesse Orosco held on and recorded the final out to send the Mets to the World Series for the first time in 13 years. The Mets were finally back in the Fall Classic.

It truly felt like another miracle!

The Mets opponent from the Junior Circuit would be a team trying to break a curse, a product of their complicated relationship with the OTHER New York team. The Boston Red Sox also had a very familiar pitcher on their staff: Tom Seaver. Even though he was injured, he had the chance to exact revenge on the team and fans that once loved him. (Luckily, that never came to pass.). The Sox also had two of the best players in the game in a young phenom, Roger Clemens and the dangerous Wade Boggs. This was really going to be a Fall "Classic"!

The first two games were to be played at Shea. Mets fans were super-energized to see their team back in the World Series. In Game 1, the Mets sent Ron Darling to face Red Sox ace Bruce Hurst. They matched each other pitch for pitch - a pitchers' duel for most of the night. So much so that after six innings the score was still 0-0. Then, Sox Catcher Rich Gedman hit a ball that went through Tim Teufel's legs and into center field which scored Jim Rice from second base to give Boston a 1-0 lead. Unfortunately for the Mets, they were unable to tie the game and dropped the opener of the series, 1-0.

Game 2 was a dream matchup as both teams' young stars, Roger Clemens of Boston and the Mets' Dwight Gooden, faced off against each other. Fans were sure they were in for another pitchers' duel. The Red Sox had other ideas as Boston was able to put up three runs in the top of the third inning to take a 3-0 lead. The Mets would rally back to cut the deficit to just one run in the bottom half of the third. Unfortunately, the Sox would end any hope that the Mets might have had to come all the way back when, in the top of the fourth, Dave Henderson hit a home run to right, making it 4-2. Boston would tack on 5 more runs and run away with Game 2 by the score of 9-3. All of a sudden, the optimism that the Mets fans had harbored before the series was fading after losing the first two at home - and fading fast. Knowing that the next three games would be played at Fenway Park in Boston, many wondered if the Mets season-long run was going to come to an abrupt end.

Game 3 featured a former Red Sox pitcher in Bobby Ojeda going for the Mets while the Red Sox went with the reliable "Oil Can" Boyd. The Mets desperately wanted to avoid the Sox taking a commanding 3-0 lead in the series. They finally got a lead in a game when they exploded for a four-run first inning and never looked back. Behind a great pitching performance from Ojeda, the Blue and Orange won decisively in Game 3, 7-1, to get back in the series now only trailing 2 games to 1.

New York went back to Ron Darling for Game 4 while the Sox went with Al Nipper who matched Darling with zeros until the top of the 4th inning, when Gary Carter hit a two-run home run over the Green Monster in left field to give the Mets the lead. Carter would go on to hit another home run later in the game. Behind Darling's scoreless seven innings while giving up only 4 hits, the Mets would go on to win Game 4, 6-2, tying the series up at two games apiece. The Mets and their fans now realized that if they won Game 5, they could wrap up the series at home and win another world championship! They could almost taste it…

However, the Red Sox had other plans. They proceeded to take control in Game 5 off of several fielding errors by the Mets and chipped away at starter Dwight Gooden. Sox starter Bruce Hurst was dominant, twirling a complete game victory, to send the series back to Shea with Boston one win away from taking it all. The Mets needed to win the final two games. They were hoping to feed off of their crowd and get off to a good start like they had in games 3 and 4.

The teams traded runs through eight innings and forced Game six to go to extras. All the Mets needed was to give up no runs in the top of the 10th and then score just one in the bottom half to force a Game 7. The Red Sox, however, were able to score two runs to take a 5-3 lead going into the bottom of the 10th. After Wally Backman and Keith Hernandez flew out to start the inning, the Mets found themselves one out away from losing the World Series, helping the Sox end their title drought of (at that point) 68 years, burying the "Curse of The Bambino". All hope seemed lost, and the Mets looked like they were

1986

going to have to deal with another major disappointment in the history of this franchise. The outlook wasn't brilliant.

When all of a sudden, then the Winds of Shea began blowing in the opposite direction…

8

The Second Miracle

Mets' Catcher Gary Carter got a base hit to left field to keep the Mets alive. Then, rookie Kevin Mitchell followed that with a base hit of his own to center to put the tying run on base. Up stepped Ray Knight who hit a bloop to center that allowed Carter to score. The Mets now had a chance to tie the game with Mitchell at third base. The Sox knew it was time to bring in Bob Stanley to get the one out that they still needed to win the World Series. He faced Mookie Wilson who got down to his final strike. Once again the Mets found themselves with only one shot left to keep the series alive.

Mookie fouled off a few pitches, and Stanley missed outside to bring the count to 2-2. Then, on the ninth pitch of the at bat, Stanley threw a fastball low and inside that got past the catcher, all the way to the backstop. Mitchell scored from third with the tying run. Incredibly, the Mets had come back, scoring two runs to tie the game, all while being down to their last out. The inning wasn't over just yet! The Red Sox still needed the final out to force another extra inning.

On the tenth and final pitch of the at bat, Wilson hit a little roller down the first base line, and Vin Scully made the most iconic calls in Mets history: "Little roller up along first. Behind the bag! It gets through Buckner! Here comes Knight, and the Mets win it!"

The Mets somehow had prevailed in Game 6, forcing a decisive Game 7, at home! The stars seemingly were aligning in the Mets favor. - They were one win away from coming back to win a world championship…

Game 7 would feature Bruce Hurst and Ron Darling for the third time in the series. The Red Sox finally were able to solve Darling's pitching by grabbing three runs in the top of the second inning and kept that lead halfway through the game. Once again, the Mets' hopes seemed to be evaporating. However, these Mets were resilient and wouldn't go quietly in the New York "Knight". In the bottom of the 6th inning, the Mets loaded the bases for Keith Hernandez. He came through with a two-run double to cut the deficit to 3-2, giving the team life. Gary Carter then followed with a bloop to right field that Red Sox' outfielder Dwight Evans couldn't get, scoring another run to tie the game at three. The Mets had done it again!

    Then, in the bottom of the seventh inning, Ray Knight came up and hit a towering drive to right field. It looked gone, it felt gone, it sounded gone…IT **WAS** GONE! The Mets had taken a 4-3 lead with just six outs to go! Two more runs would score later in the inning to make it 6-3, giving the Mets some breathing room. The Red Sox, however, would score two in the eighth to make it 6-5,

The Second Miracle

keeping their chances alive. But Darryl Strawberry dashed any hopes of a comeback for Boston when he hit his first home run of the series in the bottom of the eighth. The Mets would add another run that inning to go into the 9th up 8-5. The Mets were three outs away - Three!

Mets' closer Jesse Orosco went 3-up-3 down in the ninth and the New York Mets were World Champions once more! The Mets had become only the second team in MLB history (up until that point) to come back to win the World Series after losing the first two games. After 17 grueling years, the Blue and Orange were the best in baseball.

Just like in '69 New York City had a ticker-tape parade for the club and no one was happier than World Series MVP Ray Knight who became a Mets legend with his clutch performances in Game 6 and 7. Some fans had worried that they would never see the Mets win again, but here they were, in 1986, World Series Champions!

Meet the Mets

It looked like there would be a parade like this for many years to come. And yet, something was missing…

9

Sour Apples

…Or rather, someONE…

While the team and and its delirious fans were celebrating, there was one important figure that wasn't anywhere to be seen: Dwight Gooden. Which brings up the question, Why?? A pitcher who had already won a Rookie of the Year, a CY Young AND a World Series ring to not be at the most important celebration of all? The answer is simple, one simple word: Drugs.

Gooden spent the entire evening following the Mets winning the World Series out on the town and missed the parade the next day. None of his teammates knew where he was or what had happened to him. We have to remember that in the 80's, drugs were extremely popular. Particularly crack cocaine and alcohol. New York City was the biggest playground for drugs and it was easy for basically anyone to get them - and get hooked. Unfortunately for Gooden, he did both. Drugs were not the only dreaded D-word in Dwight's life - clearly, he had his demons. Demons that, as he demonstrated, kept him down. This dynamic (if devilish) duo of drugs would go on to dog him for the rest of his all-too-short, shoulda-been-Hall-Of-Fame career.

He would eventually be found, and even though he had missed out on the parade, the Mets organization felt that it wouldn't be the last time they would have one. After all, they had a team led by some of the best players in the game at that point. Two in Gooden and Strawberry who were stars in the making. For sure, so the thinking went, the Mets would not only get back to multiple World Series, but win them as well.

The Mets did win 92 games in '87, but were denied a chance to defend their World Series crown, finishing just

Sour Apples

3 games back of the St. Louis Cardinals for the division, and missed the playoffs. You could start to see that things were unraveling a little inside the covering. None the less, in '88 the team bounced back, winning 100 games, the National League East title and a NLCS matchup with the Los Angeles Dodgers- a team that had won only 94 games.

The Mets had come back from a 3-2 deficit in the series to force Game 7 in LA, but unfortunately, the ride ended there, as the Mets were shut out 6-0. Their hopes of making it back to the World Series were dashed. Many began to wonder why this was happening. A team that was just two years removed from winning it all was now reverting back to a team that couldn't get it done. Again - Why?? Again that one word answer: Drugs.

You see, Gooden wasn't the only one with demons. There was another mega star that raised the Apple only to have it go sour. Darryl Strawberry, the man with the beautiful, near perfect swing, was also wrestling with drugs. He, too, had become hooked on the the glitzy night life of New York City in the '80s. Even the veteran presence of Keith Hernandez couldn't prevent the downfall of the team. He himself had become engulfed in it, that one disastrous maelstrom: Drugs.

Things continued to spiral out of control after '88, so much so that the team began to move on from its core, some would say, its soul. Doc and Darryl eventually were gone, with Strawberry becoming a Dodger in '91 via free agency and Gooden being released in '94. The Mets did try to compensate by getting Vince Coleman in '91. Coleman was coming off leading the NL in stolen bases for six consecutive years. Talk about hot! It seemed like an exciting way to make up for the tragic decline of their former superstars. But instead, he actually contributed at least to Doc's decline. Seems that while swinging a golf club in the clubhouse he injured Gooden's arm. And then, just a few months later he would become embroiled in a firecracker-tossing incident outside Dodger Stadium that left three people injured.

According to the Baltimore Sun, a 33-year-old woman, an 11-year-old boy, and a 2-year-old girl were all treated at local hospitals with various injuries. The 2-year-old got the worst of it as she suffered an eye injury and burns to her cheek. The family later filed a lawsuit.

Although he apologized for the incident and claimed that he didn't throw the firecracker in the direction of the fans, numerous eyewitnesses refuted his account. The two-time All-Star faced up to three years in prison but was able to get a sentence of 200 hours of community service instead. Coleman played his final game for the Mets one week after the incident and was traded at the end of the season.

Just ten years removed from the last World Series, the Mets were once again at the bottom of baseball's totem pole. It seemed that there was no hope in sight, that this franchise was doomed to be under dark clouds for many decades to come…

Sour Apples

Meet the Mets

10

A Light - in the "Piazza"

By the end of the 1996 season, the Mets were clearly in the throes of mediocrity once again. That season, they finished 20 games below .500 at 71-91 - the team's 6th straight losing season, dating back to 1991. The 1986 World Championship now seemed like eons ago. Mets fans were looking for something, ANYTHING, to grasp onto in the hope that one day their club would become good again…

Then, in 1997, they were thrown an unexpected lifeline. Mets principal owners Nelson Doubleday Jr. and Fred Wilpon decided to go in a new direction. They fired general manager Joe McIlvaine in the middle of '97 and promoted Steve Phillips to become the full-time GM. They also hired Bobby Valentine as the new manager.

Valentine was a former Met who had been the bench coach for Dallas Green before Green was fired with 31 games left in the '96 season.

At first, these moves did not give Mets fans warm feelings. After all, Phillips was unproven as a GM and Valentine had had very little success as a manager with the Texas Rangers prior to coming to New York. However, both men got off to a very good start in their respective roles.

Led by veterans Todd Hundley, John Olerud, Carlos Baerga, Carl Everett, and Bobby Jones the Mets had an incredible turnaround season winning 17 more games than the previous year, finishing the season with a winning record of 88-74. Even though they missed out on postseason play by just a few games, the team was starting to go in the right direction. Just a few more changes needed to be made to get them over the hump.

The dawning of the 1998 season saw them field a solid

team, with the addition of third baseman Edgardo Alfonzo, utility man Matt Franco, and starter Al Leiter to the fold. Even still, the papers in New York had dubbed them "A nice little team" that was on the rise. However, the team knew it needed that superstar to really take them to the next level, on the field and in the minds of the press.

And then, on May 22, 1998 they found a light in the Piazza. Mike Piazza. Piazza, arguably one of the best players in baseball at that point, was made available by the Florida Marlins after they had acquired him a week earlier from the Dodgers due to a major contract dispute. Mets GM Steve Phillips knew he had to get Piazza. He did just that, trading Preston Wilson, Ed Yarnell and Geoff Goetz to the Marlins. The Mets had found their superstar.

Piazza didn't show it early on in his Mets tenure, getting off to a slower than hoped-for start. With Free Agency looming, many wondered if his time in New York would be short lived. Then, all of the sudden, Piazza and the Mets began to click. Piazza went on a tear for the rest of the season and finished batting .348 with 23 home runs and 76 RBI's in just over 100 games to end the season. Even though the team finished with an identical 88-74 record as the previous year and missed the playoffs, the Mets knew that this team was now poised to take that next step.

In the offseason however, Mets part-owner Fred Wilpon was reluctant to sign Piazza to the biggest contract in baseball, leading many fans to fear Piazza would leave. But Nelson Doubleday would have none of it. He demanded the Wilpons agree to sign the superstar catcher, being quoted by the New York Times saying, "How could you not afford to?". Eventually the Wilpons agreed and the Mets signed Mike Piazza to a 7-year, $91 Million Dollar contract. Piazza was here to stay.

In 1999 the Mets really took off. Led by Piazza,

Meet the Mets

Olerud, Rickey Henderson, and Robin Ventura, the Mets won 97 games en route to making the playoffs as the National League Wild Card team. They faced the Arizona Diamondbacks, champions of the National League West, in the NLDS and beat them 3 games to none. They finished the series off in dramatic fashion when Todd Pratt hit a walk-off home run in Game 4. That sent the Mets to the Championship Series of the National League - where they would face the League's team of the 90's, the perennial powerhouse Atlanta Braves.

The series got off to a terrible start during which the Mets went down 3-0 in the series. Then, the they embarked on the near impossible. The Mets battled back to win Game 4 to keep the series alive. In Game 5, looking to send it back to Atlanta down only 3-2, Robin Ventura came up with the bases loaded needing only a hit to keep the Mets hopes alive. He did more than that as he proceeded to hit the ball deep into right center field in the bottom of the 15th. MLB broadcaster Gary Thorne said it best, "Robin Ventura, the Mets win 4-3, there will be a Game 6!"

Incredibly, the Mets had gone from down 3-0 in the series to being one win away from forcing a game 7. The magic continued in Game 6 when the Mets battled back from down 5-0 to tie the game up at 7 going into the 8th inning. Alas, the Mets would eventually run out of that magic and the Braves were able to win the game in the bottom of the 11th and advance to the World Series.

It was a gut-wrenching loss, no doubt. It was also the end of the 20th century. The Mets were determined to kick off the 21st Century with a season to remember.

Meet the Mets

11

2000

Going into the new century and new year of 2000, the Mets knew that they needed more pieces if they were to go deeper in October. Towards that end, they signed third baseman Todd Zeile to improve the infield as well as to put another clutch bat in the lineup. They acquired Derek Bell and Mike Hampton in a trade with the Houston Astros. Another interesting move was buying Timo Perez' contract from Hiroshima of the Japan Central league, thereby adding speed on the bases.

With those additions, the Mets became a more-feared team in the National League. Their lineup included not just Piazza but also the talents of Edgardo Alfonzo, Robin Ventura, and even the surprising Benny Agbayani. Their pitching rotation was certainly deep now with the likes of

2000

Hampton, Al Leiter and Bobby Jones. (Fun fact: The staff also included one Patrick Mahomes - no, not THAT Patrick Mahomes, but his well- traveled, savvy veteran Old Man!). The Mets were a team on a mission, not to just get to the World Series, but to win it.

Right from Opening Day, the Mets came out like a house on fire, dominating the opposition all season long. They finished with the third-best record in the National League at 94-68, trailing only the perennial NL East champion Atlanta Braves and the West champion San Francisco Giants. Piazza and Alfonzo carried the batting load with MVP-caliber seasons. Alfonzo hit .324 with 25 home runs and 94 RBIs. Not to be outdone, Piazza also finished at .324, but clubbed 38 home runs, knocking in 113 RBIs. Mike Hampton and Al Leiter won a combined 31 games at the top of the rotation. The Mets were ready for another run at the postseason - one they were determined would last deep into October and not end until they brought home the Commissioner's Trophy.

In the NLDS, they faced the team with the best record in baseball during the regular season, the 97-65 Giants. The Mets were considered clear underdogs in this series, and it looked that way after they dropped Game 1. However, the team did not give up and won the next 3 games in shocking fashion to win the series, advancing to the National League Championship Series. The Mets were just 4 wins away from going back to the Fall Classic.

In the NLCS, the Blue and Orange matched up with the red and white of the St. Louis Cardinals, who had upset the defending NL champion Atlanta Braves in their half of the NLDS. The Mets would have their hands full. However, the team was confident and it showed, with them garnering a split of the first two games in St. Louis. They were led by Timo Perez' NLCS-tying record of 8 runs scored as well as great performances from Mike Hampton (who would be named NLCS MVP). The Mets won the next three games at Shea and punched their ticket to the World Series for the first time in 14 years. It wasn't as much of a miracle as times before, but the feeling was still sweet, as sweet as the Apple in center field.

Their opponent in the World Series was the one that many thought they'd never see. One that put the whole world of baseball's focus squarely on New York City. That opponent was the Mets' cross-town rival, the team of the 90's, winners of three out of the last four World Series and looking for a third in a row, the hated New York Yankees. Led by the Fab Five of Bernie Williams, Derek Jeter, Andy Pettitte, Jorge Posada and the great Mariano Rivera, the Bronx Bombers came into The Series having faced much adversity during the season.

Or rather, during September. They had had their usual very good regular season - until September. That month they struggled to win games, losing 14 of their last 17 and finishing with an uninspiring 87-75 mark. They had been pushed to the brink of elimination in the Division Series vs. Oakland and then fought hard against the talented Seattle Mariners team, going on to win the LCS in 6 games. Thus the stage was set for the first Subway Series since the '56 Fall Classic (in which the Yankees ominously defeated the Brooklyn Dodgers in 7 games).

Even though this WAS the Yankees, the Mets, as well as many others, felt that THEY were the favorites. This was their chance to prove not only who was the best team in all of baseball in 2000, but who really was The King of New York.

2000

12

The Sub (par) Way Series

"I'll say five games, And we're going to win it."

To say that the Mets were confident going into the Fall Classic might be an understatement. All of the Mets players felt super confident that not only could they just win the series, but they would dominate. One such player on the team felt so confident that he made it public to the whole world how he felt the series would go. Mets' outfielder Benny Agbayani was interviewed on two separate shows asking him his thoughts on the upcoming series. He first spoke with Howard Stern, the shock-jock (during which interview he made that brash prediction.

"You believe that?" Stern asked.

"Yeah."

"You believe that?"

"Yeah."

If that were not clear enough, later on that day, Agbayani again was asked to give his prediction, this time with "Live" host Regis Philbin.

"What's your prediction, buddy?" Philbin asked Agbayani.

"Mets in five," Agbayani said.

"Talk about confidence," Regis quipped. "I'm a Yankee fan, but I tip my hat to you guys."

Clearly Agbayani was not short on confidence. However, there was another big reason why the Mets were so self-assured going into the Series - the first "Subway Series" in 44 years.

That reason was the pressure that Yankees owner George Steinbrenner put on his team to win the Series - not just ANY World Series, but THIS one. To say he disliked the Mets would be putting it mildly. He hated them. An indication of such enmity could be seen two years later, during a spring training game at the self-named George M. Steinbrenner Field in Tampa. The son of fan favorite and perennial World Series hero - Andy Pettitte - had his picture taken in the Yankees' dugout while wearing a Mets hat. It turns out the Mets were the name of his Little League team. Steinbrenner was so enraged that he kicked Pettitte's son out of the dugout.

Out of all the teams in baseball, the last one that he wanted to lose to in the World Series was the Mets. If they were to be bested by their inner-city rival, it would be such a loss of face, turning the City into a Mets town. It was like in the 80s, when the Yankees were experiencing an unprecedented virtually decade-long championship drought, while the Mets were perennial playoff contenders. That was intolerable enough - but if the Mets climbed to the mountaintop over the Yankees… So there was a lot on the line for both teams. You knew that this World Series would have the makings of a classic.

The Sub (par) Way Series

Game 1 took place in the Bronx. The Mets came out and were delivering on their swagger, leading 3-2 going into the bottom of the 9th. They were 2 outs away from a huge victory at Yankee Stadium. A 1-0 lead in the Series would be HUGE. Then up stepped Yankees' outfielder Paul O'Neill - nicknamed by none other than Steinbrenner himself, "The Warrior". O'Neill got down 1-2 in the count. He fouled off the next pitch. Then the next. Then the next. THEN THE NEXT. It seemed like he had two strikes against him forever. Eventually he got the count full, resulting in a 1-out walk to put the tying run on base.

The Yanks would go on to tie the game in that inning, eventually winning it in the 12th inning on a Jose Vizcaino RBI single. The Mets had victory firmly in their jaws, putting a stranglehold on the Fall Classic, getting at least a split if not a sweep of the vaunted Yankees in their hallowed home park…. When the dust settled, they instead found themselves down 1-0 in the Series.

Meet the Mets

Though stunned, the Mets had been bloodied, but were unbowed. Game 2 started with Mike Piazza hitting a grounder, severing his bat in two. While the ball went harmlessly to short, the barrel of the bat careened directly at Yankees pitcher Roger Clemens. Clemens, in the heat of the moment, proceeded to throw the broken barrel right at Piazza, causing a confrontation for a few minutes. There was some history between Piazza and Clemens. Earlier in the year at Yankee Stadium, Clemens hit Piazza with a pitch squarely in the head that caused a tense standoff between the two. Piazza was not pleased; Clemens was not apologetic.

After that, the Mets would struggle throughout the game until the top of the 9th when they trailed 6-0. Behind home runs by Piazza and Jay Payton, the team battled back to trail by 1. Unfortunately, the Mets magic ran out and they lost the game 6-5. They were now down 2-0 in the Series, heading back to Queens.

The Sub (par) Way Series

Even still, the Mets didn't feel that it was a problem. After all, though the team was down 2-0, they knew the next 3 games would be at Shea Stadium, a place where they had rarely lost all year. Yankees manager Joe Torre - a former player and manager for the Mets - had a reason to feel uneasy going into Game 3. He was once quoted saying, "The outcome of the series will be decided by whoever wins Game 3."

He would feel that way, because in '96, his Yankees lost the first 2 games at home against the dominant Atlanta Braves- the team of the decade in the National League. The Yanks ended up coming back to sweep the next four, after taking that crucial Game 3. Torre knew the Mets would come out hungry in that first game at Shea.

Torre's worries seemed to be justified. Led by timely RBI hits from Agbayani and Todd Zeile, the Mets would win Game 3 by the score of 4-2 and were back in the

World Series. The loss irritated George Steinbrenner, so much so, that he began to obsess about little things. Before Game 4, he replaced all of the furniture and stools from the visiting clubhouse at Shea with luxury couches and setback chairs in hopes of turning the momentum around.

Fresh from their team's resounding win, Mets fans were energized and excited going into Game 4. They were ready for the team to tie this series up and really grab the advantage. When Yankee-star Derek Jeter stepped into the box to start the game, the Mets fans were in a frenzy. They were going crazy, loud as you could possibly be.

Unfortunately, Jeter took the first pitch of game to deep left field. Announcer Gary Thorne, take it away: "And he goes after the first pitch, way back left field, Derek Jeter, he's on and out! Goodbye home run! First pitch homer for Derek Jeter!" Yankees, 1-0, just like that.

The Sub (par) Way Series

All of a sudden, the wind was taken out of the Mets' - and their fans' - sails. Although they bravely battled back in the game, they lost a close one 3-2. Now they trailed a worrisome 3-1, going into Game 5.

The Mets were now staring in the eyes the possibility of losing three straight games in the World Series at home. And to the hated Yankees! In Game 5, the teams matched each other pitch for pitch, a good old fashioned pitchers' duel. The game felt like it would go on all night. It certainly seemed that way going into the top of the 9th. Mets' pitcher Al Leiter had well over 100 pitches, but was still battling strong.

The Yanks, however, got two runners on with two men out. Up stepped the little-heralded Luis Sojo. He had started the season with the lowly Pittsburgh Pirates, having no hopes of reaching the playoffs, much less World Series glory. Leiter was one strike away from getting out of the jam still tied. On his 142nd pitch of the night, Sojo hit a ball that must have bounced ten or more times, slowly up the middle for a base hit. Posada (who was actually hit by the throw to home) scored to give the Yankees the lead. Scott Brosius, hot on Posada's heels, scored on the play as well after the relay bounded off Posada and into the Mets' dugout. The most unlikely person for the Yankees had just given them a 2-run lead going into the bottom half of the 9th.

Though shaken, Mets' fans still had hope. Ya gotta believe! All they needed to do was get one man on base to allow Piazza a chance of keeping the Mets alive - a bloop and a blast. And who better to do the blasting than Piazza? They would have to do this, of course, against the great closer Mariano Rivera. After getting the first out, Agbayani came up and worked a walk to put the tying run on base. See? SEE??

After Edgardo Alfonzo flew out, the Mets found themselves down to their last out, up stepped the man of the moment, the man who had taken the team on his back all season- Mike Piazza.

This was it! This man was the reason the Mets were even in the World Series! Now with a chance to tie the game! The hero the Mets needed! And on the 2nd pitch, it looked like deliverance had come!

Piazza hits the ball to deep center field. There it is! There is the home run that will save us! Bernie Williams going back, back, back - but wait! Why is he slowing down? Doesn't he know that ball is DESTINED to land in the parking lot? Doesn't he know the Big Apple will rise behind him? What?? He's circling it off!? NO! NO! It can't be! It just can't be!!

But... It was. Bernie settles under the ball. He makes the catch. Ball game over! World Series over! Yankees win...THHHHHEEEEE YANKEES WIN!

When Bernie made the catch, you could see he didn't immediately celebrate. He knelt to one knee in prayerful thanks, a sigh of relief. Many Yankees players from that series will tell you that there wasn't much of celebration, but much more relief that they had won it all. And they avoided the wrath of the guy known to everyone as - The Boss.

Even though there were Yankees fans there, you'd hardly know it. Shea Stadium went from being in a frenzy of anticipation…to pure silence. You could hear a pin drop; it was that quiet. Mets fans just couldn't believe it.

The next day, a Mets fan called into WFAN, the New York sports talk station. He was quoted saying, "I can't go back to Shea. The place has been defiled." There was a parade through the Canyon of Heroes, but it wasn't for the team in Blue and Orange, it was once again for those…

Damn Yankees.

The Sub (par) Way Series

13
The Decade of Regrets

After the 2000 Series, many Mets fans were sure their team was well positioned to win a long line of World Series titles. With the talent the team assembled there was no way that the Mets wouldn't be back in the Fall Classic several more times. Instead of World Series though, what followed next was a series of moments that made the Mets into something more like the "Regrets".

In what felt like a snap of a finger, much of the magic and talent of the ball club seemed to disappear. From the start of the '01 season to the end of the '05 season, the Mets only had two winning seasons, and even those contained no more than 83 victories. Even still, the seeds of success were planted during this drought in 2003 when the Mets acquired one of the biggest free agent pitchers in the game - Tom Glavine, he of the perennial rival Atlanta

Braves. Glavine had put together a pretty impressive resume with Atlanta - 8-time All Star, World Series Champion, World Series MVP, 2-time CY Young winner and a 5-time leader in wins in the National League. With Glavine leading the staff, the Mets hoped to chop into the Braves' divisional dominance.

Then in 2004, the team called up their top prospect who would go on to become the greatest 3rd baseman in team history. David Wright was a kid who was tearing up the minor leagues and keen on making his mark in the majors. Through 69 games in his rookie season with the Big Club, Wright compiled a .293 batting average with 14 home runs and 40 RBI's. Mets fans were certain this kid was going to be something special.

And then the team started to bring in the right pieces to help Glavine and Wright succeed. The first was signing Pedro Martinez, who had left the reigning World Series champion Boston Red Sox in free agency, giving the Mets not one, but TWO big-name battle-proven pitchers at the top of their rotation. Then, in what was one of the biggest moves of the decade, they brought in slugging outfielder Carlos Beltran, also through free agency. He had been poised to sign with the Yankees originally, but whether it was the Baseball Gods getting revenge for the Mets from 2000 or something else, the Yankees didn't land Beltran but instead he became the King of Queens.

The Mets were now primed to go all the way and bring a championship back to Queens. The Mets dominated the regular season with 97 wins and a National League East title. They swept past the Dodgers in the NLDS, who had unaccountably tripped them up in '88, and faced the St. Louis Cardinals in the LCS, a team who won just 83 games that year.

Despite the disparity in their records, the teams battled back and forth in the series and after 6 games, it was all even at 3 games apiece. Game 7 would be played at Shea.

Mets fans believed that they would win this game and move on to the World Series - a great night for that coronation in Queens. Truly, ya gotta believe!

The game was tied at 1 after 1, and with things quieting down for the next several innings, the contest had all the makings of a back and forth duel that might go deep into the October night. That was until the top of the 6th inning. At that point, any play, any at-bat, any pitch, could be the decisive factor in the outcome. After Cardinal Jim Edmonds worked a one out walk, up stepped Scott Rolen who had struggled at the plate in this playoff year. However, on the first pitch he ripped one deep to left field. Mets fans held their breath. NO! NOT NOW! The ball was going, going… and it was...

CAUGHT!

WHAT!?!?

Endy Chavez, the Mets left fielder had leapt over the wall and robbed Rolen of a home run! And not just that -

Chavez threw the ball back into the infield for a key double play. Endy caught Edmonds halfway to third, as he - like everyone else - thought that ball was on its way out. Mets fans went insane! In a split second, the Mets had put a stranglehold on the game and were poised to take that momentum into the bottom half of the inning.

The Mets loaded the bases with two outs. Next up, who else? - the man of the hour, Endy Chavez, who just saved those two crucial runs in the top of the frame and could now give the Mets the lead in the bottom, and be the hero once more!

The first pitch was right down the freaking middle. OH! It's perfect! Chavez, with all his might swings at it, hits it in the air...right to Edmonds in medium center field to end the inning.

The home team still had the momentum and the home crowd behind them. And there were still two innings to go – and the all-important last ups. Everything will work out in the end, right? This was still their time, right?

In the top of the 9th, with both starters already done for the game, it was the bullpens that would determine the outcome. Edmonds led off, striking out but then Rolen singled to left. Up to the plate stepped St. Louis' young phenom catcher, Yadier Molina. Mets pitcher Aaron Heilman nodded to catcher Paul Lo Duca and delivered the pitch.

BOP! A drive to deep left field. NO! NOT NOW! Wait it is Chavez again, he'll catch another one and save the day again! The ball is going, going, and it is...

GONE!

WHAT!?!?

Cardinals 3, Mets 1 going to the bottom of the 9th...

The Mets however, don't go quietly into the New York night. Jose Valentin and Chavez lead off the inning with back-to-back singles. Then after two quick outs, Paul Lo Duca works a walk. And who steps into the batters' box?

Meet the Mets

The prize, the great hope, that King of Queens - Carlos Beltran. The most clutch hitter on the Mets, and maybe on the entire planet, is up with the bases loaded. With one swing of the bat, "Señor Octubre", who had proven his clutchness with the Royals and his playoff mettle with the Astros, would send the Mets to the Fall Classic.

Cardinals rookie closer Adam Wainwright knows that this is a daunting task ahead of him. The first pitch is a changeup down the middle. Beltran lets it go. Strike one. Pitch two is a curveball in the dirt, Beltran swings and misses. Strike two. Mets fans hold their breath - they still have hope, this will all work out, the Mets will win! Wainwright comes to set, he's ready, Beltran is ready. The wind up and the 0-2 pitch...

But there was to be no joy in Flushing that night...

Or for the rest of the decade, for that matter. The team of so much promise unaccountably fired manager Willie Randolph (who had nearly led them to the Series again) in a most humiliating way. The result at the end of the season would not be getting over the hump, but instead the Collapse of 2007.

And if that were not bad enough, it was followed by the Collapse of 2008.

The Mets ended the decade finishing 4th in their division, twenty two games under .500, as they limped towards the 2010s…

14

A New Hope...?

Going into the 2010's, many Mets fans were hopeful that the new decade would create new, positive memories for the franchise. After all, in 2010, the team was going into its 2nd season in their beautiful new ballpark, Citi Field, after the team had moved across the parking lot from Shea Stadium (which was unceremoniously razed to become the NEW parking lot). The team also had a good nucleus of talent on the roster, starting with the pitching duo of Johan Santana and R.A. Dickey. With the bat, the Mets had the dynamic duo of David Wright and Jose Reyes at 3rd Base and Shortstop, respectively. With a solid club, the team was ready to compete for a pennant - as well as rid the ghosts of recent season failures past.

Unfortunately, the exact opposite transpired, with a

disappointing 79-83 record in 2010. After that season, the Mets made a bunch of drastic moves with the hope that they could become relevant again. They brought back Carlos Beltran, not just to help with performance on the field, but to bring some fans back to the stadium. The Mets also hoped to repair bridges that they had burned with Beltran after his previous exit. To add to the mix, Jason Bay and Lucas Duda were brought in to put more pop in the bat. But none of those expected things happened, and once again the Mets finished below .500 at 77-85.

And contrary to the attempts at fixing bridges - Beltran was gone again by mid-season - the Mets continued to burn them with other players as well. One in particular was with fan-favorite Jose Reyes in 2012. Reyes was a free agent and decided to leave the Mets to join the rival and upstart Miami Marlins. The main reason for this was that the Mets were not willing to give Reyes the money he wanted. Mets fans were enraged by this and were crushed to see such an important and beloved star leave. After that, the Mets would go on to have 3 more losing seasons, with none of them producing more than 79 wins. For what seemed like the umpteenth time, the Mets were in the basement, not just of the National League, but of Major League baseball itself. Many wondered if they would ever become even just competitive again. Little did they know that in 2015, the team, as well as the city they played in, would go on a magical ride that would be unlike anything they had recently experienced.

While the Big Club was struggling, the farm system was developing a crop of talented, young players. The most noticeable area of this was the pitching staff. It started with the emergence of Matt Harvey. The "Dark Knight" - as he would later be nicknamed - was going into just his 2nd full season with the Mets and already had shown a lot of promise, looking to become the ace of the

A New Hope…?

staff. As good as Harvey was, however, the ace proved to be the Degrom-inantor - right hander Jacob DeGrom. He flourished in 2014 and earned a full-time starting role going into 2015. Then came a pitcher that with his superhero velocity could save the Mets universe from evil. - Noah "Thor" Syndergaard was acquired by the Mets a few years prior in a what had appeared at the time to be the head scratcher trade of R.A. Dickey, the Cy Young award winner for the Mets in 2012. Thor's very impressive Spring Training convinced the Mets to put him on the big league roster to start 2015. The last addition was a tall, lengthy southpaw who came up mid-way through the season. He also grew up not too far from New York City in Stony Brook. His name was Steven Matz and he had the uncanny ability to get hitters to ground into double plays.

Amazin'ly, the Mets had comprised an entire rotation with up-incoming aces, in a single season. As for the offense, they still had David Wright, who despite injuries slowing him down, was still super-productive. They added Curtis Granderson as well as young, talented outfielder Michael Conforto, and the speedy duo of Juan Lagares and Ruben Tejada.

Then there was Wilmer Flores, who, in what would prove to be a pivotal series versus the Washington Nationals, would hit a walk off home run to help sweep that series and take the lead in the NL East just after the trade deadline. That had to be all the more satisfying to Flores, who, just before that deadline, got word in the dugout that he had been traded to Milwaukee. This greatly upset the emotional Flores, who could not hold in tears of disappointment. Lucky for him - and, as it would turn out, the Mets - the deal fell through due to the Brewers' Carlos Gomez failing his physical.

However, the Mets knew they needed one more piece to put this team over the hump. They got more than that

A New Hope...?

when they acquired All-Star Outfielder Yoenis Céspedes from the Detroit Tigers for mid-tier prospects. He was able to make the Mets offense that much more formidable and, as a result, the team finished with record of 90-72, clinching their first division title since the ill-fated 2006 season.

Unbelievably, the Mets had turned it around and were going to the postseason for the first time in nearly a decade. They faced the favored Los Angeles Dodgers in the NLDS, but the team battled to win the series in five games. They were now just 4 wins away from the unthinkable. They faced the Chicago Cubs in the NLCS where they dominated right from the beginning. The Mets won the first three games, taking a 3-0 lead in the series. By this point, one Met was having not just a career postseason, but one that Mets fans would remember for years to come. Daniel Murphy, who, out of nowhere, became the second-coming of Babe Ruth in the playoffs.

Meet the Mets

He tied the record for the most games in a row with a home run, with 5. Murphy became the talk of the sports world. He would continue his hot hitting in Game 4 with another home run to set a new MLB record, surpassing former teammate Beltran's previous achievement.

That home run would help propel the Mets to win the NLCS. The Mets had done it! In a season that no one expected, the New York Mets were National League Champions! They were going to the World Series for the first time in fifteen years!

Their opponent in the Fall Classic was a team who had just lost in the Series the year before in heartbreaking fashion and were looking to redeem themselves. Even though the Kansas City Royals had more experience, Mets fans really believed that they were the better team and, with the magic they had had all year long, there was no doubt it would carry into the World Series. The Mets were ready to finally reclaim the title of World

A New Hope...?

Champions again.

Meet the Mets

Epilogue: The R-E-G-R-E-T-S of New York Town

Alas, it was not to be. The Mets improbable run ended in that Fall Classic. Despite the fact that the Mets had a lead late in each game, they were only able to muster one victory, on the way to losing the Series in five games. What made it all the more regrettable were two things. The first was the hitting of the Mets, or, rather lack thereof, especially with the hero of the playoff series leading up to the Fall Classic - Daniel Murphy - going cold. The other was fielding - crucial errors were made late in games 4 and 5. Regardless of that, it was still a tough pill to swallow for Mets fans. So close, but not close enough.

Even though the Mets didn't win the World Series that year, fans were still excited about the future of the team.

With the incredible pitching staff and (normally) solid hitting, the team seemed, once again, poised to compete for championships for years to come. Unfortunately, that wasn't the case. As I am writing this book, just five years removed from the Fall Classic, the Mets, in many ways have been a great disappointment. How did they get to this point?

Well, it started with Daniel Murphy and Travis d'Arnaud leaving after 2017 via Free Agency. Since then, at least in d'Arnaud's case, he has found resurgence in his career once he left Queens. And Murphy became one of the premier hitters in the league, batting over or near .300 in each of the following non-COVID seasons. The next hit the team took was that the Captain - David Wright - was never able to truly get back to 100% form. Despite pushing through the pain, he was finally forced to retire after the 2018 season, not having played a game since 2016.

Epilogue: The R-E-G-R-E-T-S of New York Town

Then there was the glittering prize - Yoenis Céspedes... After receiving a hefty contract from the Mets in 2016, he went on to be continuously injured. That string of injuries kept him off the field for nearly the entirety of his contract. It didn't help that the relationship between Yoenis and Mets management went down the drain. It was so bad that early on in the 2020 season, Céspedes unceremoniously packed up his things and left the team, without formally informing management, never to return. (In farcical fashion, his whereabouts were unknown for several days...)

However, the hardest thing to deal with for Mets fans was the demise of the highly touted pitching staff.

Matt Harvey was the first to go. The "Dark Knight" never seemed to reclaim that 2015 form. Whether it was the late nights on the town or that hitters started to figure him out is still a mystery to this day. Harvey was traded to the Reds in 2018 after he had been designated for assignment earlier in that year. Harvey still has never been the same.

Steven Matz was next. Despite the fact that he has remained a Met since 2015 he, just like Harvey, was never able to be as successful as he was in the '15 run. Matz would occasionally show glimpses of turning a corner, but he would always fall back down. Things have gotten so bad for Matz that he was removed from the starting rotation and is now primarily used as just another bullpen arm.

Noah Syndergaard has kept his solid form for a few more years after, but just like many other Mets, injuries have slowed him down and he has since struggled to be the same "Thor" that Mets fans grew accustomed to seeing. He has not started full time for the Mets since early 2019.

The only one of the four that (at least for now) has avoided regression is Jacob DeGrom. He has continued to

Epilogue: The R-E-G-R-E-T-S of New York Town

be the "DeGrominator" after 2015. In many ways, he has become arguably the best pitcher in the National League. In the past five years, DeGrom has made the All Star Game three times, won ten or more games four times, led the Majors in ERA with a 1.70 in 2018. He was a two-time National League Cy Young Award winner, capturing the award in back-to-back years in 2018 and 2019. With perhaps more to come...

For Mets fans, there hasn't been much to be happy or hopeful for in these last few seasons. However, things might be taking a turn for the better. Billionaire and die-hard Mets fan

- Steve Cohen- finally bought the team from the Wilpons, after months of high drama involving the likes of celebrities J-Lo and A-Rod. With his promise of spending millions of dollars right away to make the team a championship contender, there is no telling what the Mets will bring to the city of New York in the future.

Ya gotta believe…

Will a change in ownership be the magic elixir? Time will tell. All Mets fans hope for is that Cohen succeeds, and doesn't bring to the franchise, and its fans, more R-E-G-R-E-T-S…

www.ingramcontent.com/pod-product-compliance
Lightning Source LLC
Chambersburg PA
CBHW032004080426
42735CB00007B/509